ST. MATTHEW'S SCHOOL
3316 SANDRA LANE
VIRGINIA BEACH, VA. 23464
757-420-2455

S0-DOQ-274

The World Wide WEB

The

World Wide WEB

Christopher Lampton

A First Book

Franklin Watts
A DIVISION OF GROLIER PUBLISHING

NEW YORK   LONDON   HONG KONG   SYDNEY
DANBURY, CONNECTICUT

Note to Readers: Terms defined in the glossary are *italicized* in the text.

Photographs ©: America Online, Inc., 1996: 17, 55; CERN, 1996: 14; Excite Inc., 1996: 42; LucasArts Entertainment, 1996: 35; Microsoft Corporation, 1996: 20; Musée du louvre, 1996: 49; Courtesy of NASA: 6, 25, 28, 29; National Broadcasting Company, 1996: 13; Courtesy of National Wildlife Federation: 11; Netscape Communications Corp., 1996: 19, 35; Courtesy of Oakland University: 31; Smithsonian Institution, 1996: 46, 47; Time Inc. New Media, 1996: 8; TVNow, 1996: 55; Courtesy of University of Michigan Web team: 32; Courtesy of the White House: 50; WSI Corp., 1996: 53; YAHOO!, Inc., 1996: 38-40, 43; Zoological Society of San Diego Library: 22, 23.

Library of Congress Cataloging-in-Publication Data

Lampton, Christopher.
    The World Wide Web / by Christopher Lampton.
        p. cm. — (A First book)
    Includes bibliographical references and index.
    Summary: A description of the World Wide Web, including the history of its development and details on how to use it.
    ISBN 0-531-20262-3 (lib.bdg.)   0-531-15842-x pbk.)
    1. World Wide Web (Information retrieval system)—Juvenile literature.
[1. World Wide Web (Information retrieval system)]
I. Title. II. Series.
TK5105.888.L36   1997
025.04—DC20   96-36145
                                         CIP
                                         AC

Copyright © 1997 by Christopher Lampton
All rights reserved. Published simultaneously in Canada
Printed in the United States of America
3 4 5 6 7 8 9 10 R 06 05 04 03 02 01 00

Contents

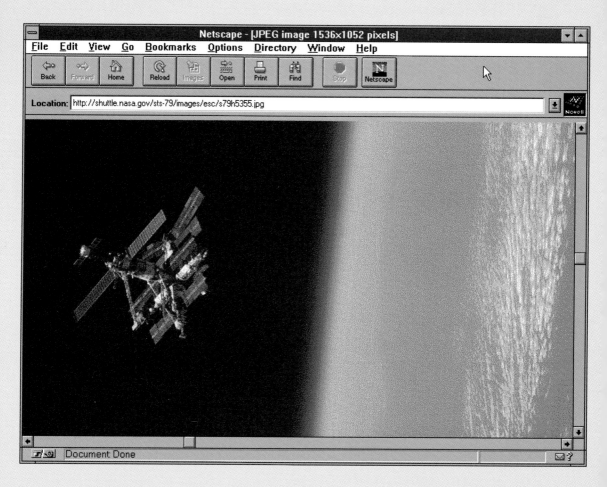

This photo, taken by astronauts on the Space Shuttle *Atlantis*, shows the space station Mir with the earth in the background. This site, located at **http://shuttle.nasa.gov/**, is one of the many exciting places to visit on the World Wide Web.

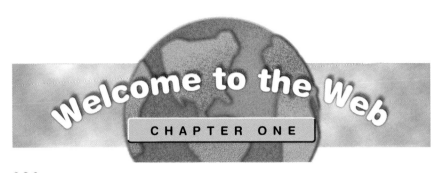

Welcome to the Web

CHAPTER ONE

Would you like to go to a place where you can see scenes from the latest movies, play games with people from all around the world, and get free versions of brand new computer programs?

If you go to this place, you might meet characters from the latest cartoons, hear samples of songs that haven't even come out yet, or learn the news before it appears on TV. Or, if you prefer, you can browse through museums, admiring beautiful paintings or statues of dinosaurs. You can look out the window of the space shuttle, listen to radio stations on the other side of the country, and even collect photographs of your favorite TV stars.

What is this place? It's called the *World Wide Web*. Like a giant book, the Web is full of pictures and words, but you'll find a lot of things you've never seen in a book before, such as animated cartoons and computer programs. And you get there, believe it or not, through a computer.

THE INTERNET

The World Wide Web is part of the international computer network called the *Internet*. What is the Internet? In a sense, it's just a bunch of wires and cables connecting millions of computers around the world. That may not sound very exciting in itself, but the Internet allows people all over the world to exchange exciting information quickly and inexpensively. By hooking your own computer to this network of wires through the telephone lines attached to your house, or by

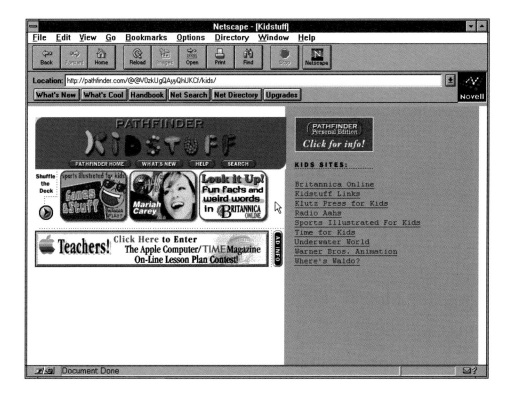

The Web can give you instant access to electronic versions of many popular magazines. At **http://pathfinder.com/**, you can browse online publications by Time, Inc., including many especially for kids.

using special computers at your school or the local library, you can connect right to the Internet yourself.

And then you can be a part of the World Wide Web!

COMPUTER FILES

Once you have a computer that's connected to the Internet, you can use special computer programs to exchange information with other computers connected to the Internet. What kind of information can you send back and forth? Anything that can be stored on a computer—documents, games, sounds, pictures, and programs—can be sent over the Internet.

All the information stored on your computer is arranged in *data files*. Your favorite computer game, the word processing program you use to type your homework, even the homework you create with that word processing program are stored in data files. The data files are recorded on the surface of a disk, which may be a portable diskette or the permanent disk inside your *hard drive*, where they can be retrieved whenever you need them.

The files you find on the Internet are exactly like the files you have on the hard drive of your computer. Like the files on your computer, they can contain many different types of information: computer programs, stories, pictures, even music. But there are more files on the Internet than you could ever fit on your computer. Remember, these files are actually kept on the hard drives of computers all around the world!

HTML FILES

One of the most important types of file on the World Wide Web is the *HTML* file. HTML is short for HyperText Markup Language. Anyone who learns this mark-up language can create HTML files, which can display pictures, play music, show animated cartoons, and—of course—contain words. To read these files on the World Wide Web, you need a computer program called a *Web browser*.

What's so special about an HTML file? The top image on the opposite page shows a picture of an HTML file as seen through a text editing program. It appears just like any *text file* you might type with a word processor—pretty boring, actually. But when you read this file with a Web browser, it looks a lot different—and a lot more interesting! The bottom image shows what this file looks like when viewed with a Web browser. The HTML file suddenly has pictures in it, and the text appears in different sizes with fancy characters. The background is even a different color. When looked at with a Web browser, an HTML file is called a *Web page*. This Web page is maintained by the National Wildlife Federation.

There are many millions of HTML files located on the Internet. When you read one or more of these files using a Web browser, you are said to be "on the World Wide Web," even if you're actually still sitting at home or at school.

WEB PAGES

The World Wide Web is made up of lots of Web pages, and they can contain other things besides pictures and text. For

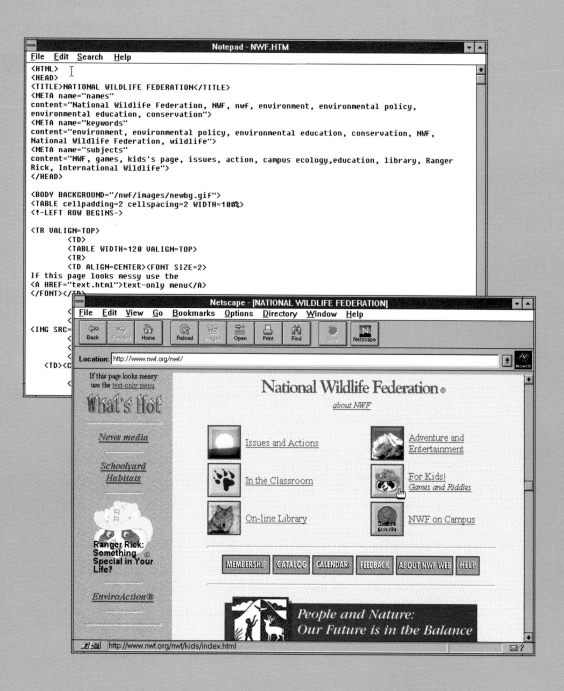

Notepad - NWF.HTM

File   Edit   Search   Help

```
<HTML>
<HEAD>
<TITLE>NATIONAL WILDLIFE FEDERATION</TITLE>
<META name="names"
content="National Wildlife Federation, NWF, nwf, environment, environmental policy,
environmental education, conservation">
<META name="keywords"
content="environment, environmental policy, environmental education, conservation, NWF,
National Wildlife Federation, wildlife">
<META name="subjects"
content="NWF, games, kids's page, issues, action, campus ecology,education, library, Ranger
Rick, International Wildlife">
</HEAD>

<BODY BACKGROUND="/nwf/images/newbg.gif">
<TABLE cellpadding=2 cellspacing=2 WIDTH=100%>
<!-LEFT ROW BEGINS->

<TR VALIGN=TOP>
        <TD>
        <TABLE WIDTH=120 VALIGN=TOP>
        <TR>
        <TD ALIGN=CENTER><FONT SIZE=2>
If this page looks messy use the
<A HREF="text.html">text-only menu</A>
</FONT></TD

<IMG SRC=

        <TD><C
```

Netscape - [NATIONAL WILDLIFE FEDERATION]

File   Edit   View   Go   Bookmarks   Options   Directory   Window   Help

Back | Forward | Home | Reload | Images | Open | Print | Find | Stop | Netscape

Location: http://www.nwf.org/nwf/

If this page looks messy use the text-only menu

What's Hot

News media

Schoolyard Habitats

Ranger Rick: Something Special in Your Life?

EnviroAction®

National Wildlife Federation ®

about NWF

Issues and Actions

In the Classroom

On-line Library

Adventure and Entertainment

For Kids! *Games and Riddles*

NWF on Campus

MEMBERSHIP | CATALOG | CALENDAR | FEEDBACK | ABOUT NWF WEB | HELP

People and Nature: Our Future is in the Balance

http://www.nwf.org/nwf/kids/index.html

instance, some Web pages contain computer programs. You can copy (or *download*) many of these programs to your computer's hard drive, just as though you had bought them in a software store. Or you can run these programs right on the Web, without leaving your browser. Still other Web pages contain sounds or music that you can listen to at the touch of a button. Some Web pages feature animated cartoons that start moving the moment the page appears on your computer screen. The pictures, cartoons, sounds, and programs are not really part of the HTML file. The HTML file simply tells your Web browser where to find all the pieces of the Web page, and the browser puts them all together.

WEB SITES

A group of Web pages put on the Web by a single person, an institution, or a company is called a *Web site*. In this book, we'll talk about a lot of Web sites, many of which have been created by major corporations or by government agencies. We'll refer to these sites by the names of those corporations or agencies. For instance, if we refer to the Web site that has been created by the NBC TV network, we'll call it the "NBC Web site." Not surprisingly, the pages on this site contain information and pictures about NBC shows and stars. The HTML files that make up this Web site are kept on a computer owned or rented by the NBC network.

The introductory page of a Web site is sometimes called the *home page*. However, this term can have other meanings

The NBC Web site

as well. For instance, a home page can also be the first page your Web browser reads off the Web when you boot it up, or it can be a page that you have created yourself. (Or it can be all of these things at the same time.)

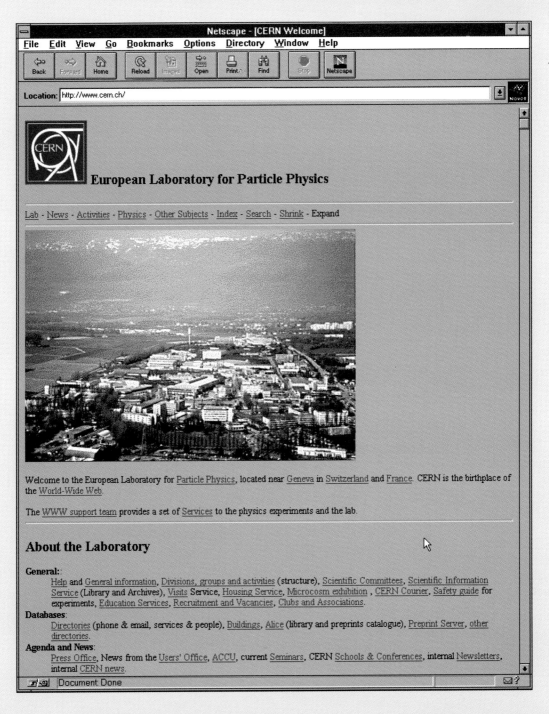

This is the home page for CERN, the birthplace of the Web.

INVENTING THE WEB

The World Wide Web was created in the early 1990s at a laboratory in Switzerland called CERN. It was intended to be a way for scientists to share information about their discoveries. In fact, until the 1990s, this was the main use of the entire Internet.

Originally, the World Wide Web contained no pictures or cartoons or sounds. Web pages contained only words. But in 1993, the first *graphical Web browser* was released—that is, a Web browser that can include pictures. It was called Mosaic, and it was given away free by programmers at the National Center for Supercomputing Applications (NCSA) at the University of Chicago. Many of the most popular Web browsers around today are based on Mosaic.

Mosaic quickly became popular even among computer users who had no interest in the scientific uses of the Web. In fact, by the mid-1990s, only a fraction of the people using the Web were scientists.

EXPLORING THE WEB YOURSELF

This book is about the World Wide Web and how you can explore Web sites with your own computer or with a computer at your school or library. In the following pages, you'll learn about some of the things that are available on the Web and how you can explore the Web yourself to find things that aren't mentioned in this book.

Getting on the Web

CHAPTER TWO

How do you get on the Web in the first place? Earlier, we said that you can get to the Web through a computer if that computer is hooked up to the Internet. If it's not, you will need to get a *modem* and contact an *Internet service provider*. And, of course, you'll need a Web browser.

MODEMS

Most computers today come with modems already installed. If your computer doesn't have a modem, you can probably buy one at your neighborhood computer store. At the time this book was written, most modems were designed to connect your computer to telephone lines. However, new ways to connect to the Internet are being invented all the time. By the time you read this book, you may be able to connect your computer to the Internet with a television cable, a digital data line, or even a satellite dish!

INTERNET SERVICE PROVIDERS

Internet service providers are companies that provide Internet connections to individuals, schools, institutions, and businesses. These companies maintain powerful computers, called *servers*, that have high-speed, permanent connections to the Internet. These computers, which run twenty-four

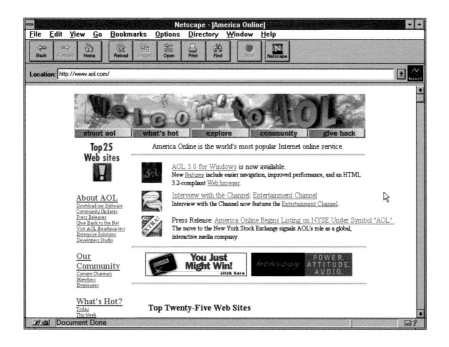

This is the home page for America Online, one of the biggest national Internet service providers. Many other companies offer Internet service to local areas. Check to see which ISP offers the best deal where you live.

hours a day, are what you connect to when you dial in to the Internet. In return for a fee, Internet service providers will give you permission to connect to the Internet through their computers. When you have this access, you are said to have an *account*.

If you don't know whether you have an account with an Internet service provider, ask a family member who knows something about computers. If you don't have an

ST. MATTHEW'S SCHOOL
3316 SANDRA LANE
VIRGINIA BEACH, VA. 23464
757-420-2455

account, ask one of your parents if it would be possible to get one. Some Internet service providers are quite inexpensive and will give you unlimited access to the World Wide Web and other Internet features for a small amount of money each month.

If you belong to one of the big online services, such as America Online or CompuServe, then you already have an Internet service provider. Just log on to the service and look for instructions on reaching the Web. Be careful, though; these companies may charge money for every minute you spend on the Internet, so it's possible to run up some pretty big bills. Make sure your parents aren't surprised.

If you can't connect to the Internet at home, you might be able to reach it for free from a computer at your school or library. Ask a teacher or a librarian about this.

GETTING A WEB BROWSER

Once you've connected to the Internet, you'll need a Web browser. You can probably get a Web browser from your Internet service provider. If you belong to an online service like America Online or CompuServe, there may even be a Web browser built into the program you ordinarily use to connect to these services.

Two of the most popular Web browsers are Netscape Navigator and Microsoft Internet Explorer. We'll use Netscape Navigator to show examples of Web pages in this book. It's a good idea to have the latest versions of these programs because they'll have extra features to help you get

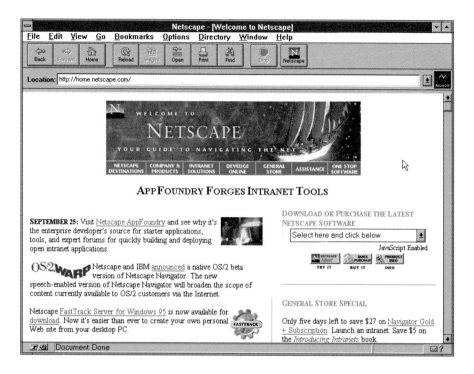

This is the home page for Netscape, maker of Netscape Navigator, which is one of the most popular Web browsers (and the one we use in this book).

the most out of the World Wide Web. Where can you get the latest versions? You can get them at your local computer store or on the World Wide Web itself! Of course, you'll need an earlier version to get onto the Web to get the latest version.

Once you've gotten a Web browser, how do you get around on the Web? This is what we'll talk about in the next chapter.

Navigating the Web

Once you have gotten a Web browser and a modem and are connected to an Internet service provider, getting onto the Web is easy. Just run your Web browser the way you'd run any other program on your computer. Most Web browsers will automatically go to the home page of the company that designed the browser. If you are using Netscape Navigator, for instance, it will go to the Netscape home page. Microsoft Internet Explorer will go to the Microsoft home page.

Once you get to those pages, you may just want to look around. There should be some interesting pictures and lots

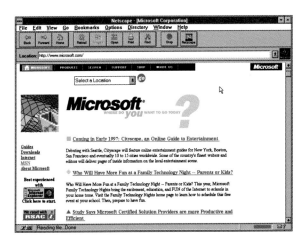

Microsoft offers a popular browser called Microsoft Internet Explorer. You can download the most recent version of the browser from Microsoft's Web site, shown here.

of information. The best part about these pages, though, is that they will contain *hyperlinks*.

HYPERLINKS

When you look at a page on the World Wide Web, you might see a word or a phrase that is underlined or in a different color from the rest of the text on the page. When you move a computer mouse pointer over the word or phrase, it changes from an arrow to a pointing hand. You can then click the mouse button.

Why would you do this? Because the word or phrase is a hyperlink, often just called a link. Some hyperlinks represent files on the Internet. These files might be other Web pages, pictures, sounds, programs—anything that can be stored on a computer. When you click on the hyperlink, the Web browser sends a message over the Internet asking to have the new file sent to your computer. When it arrives, the browser will display the new Web page, show the image, play the sound, download the program, or perform whatever action is appropriate to the type of file the hyperlink points to.

Other hyperlinks represent actions rather than files. Clicking on these links will let you send e-mail to the person in charge of a Web page or take you to another place on the same page you're reading.

Hyperlinks do not necessarily take the form of words and phrases. Sometimes, pictures are hyperlinks, and clicking on them will activate the link.

This is the Web site for the San Diego Zoo.

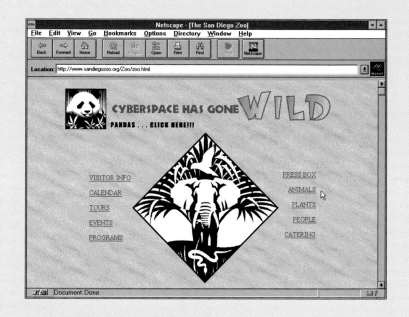

Notice that when the cursor is dragged over a link, such as ANIMALS, it changes into a pointing hand.

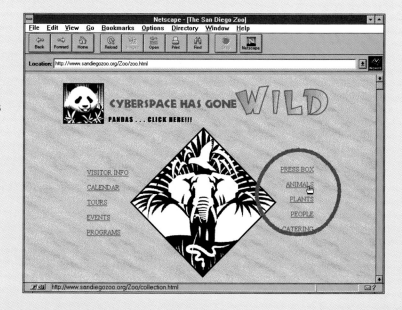

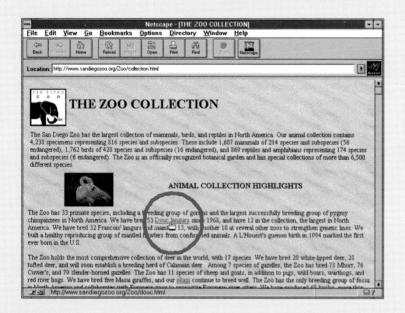

Clicking on the link brings you to this page on animals in the zoo collection. The text on this page contains more underlined links, including one that brings you to a picture of a Douc langur.

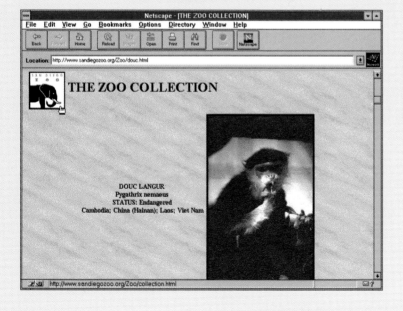

Notice that the San Diego Zoo icon at the top left corner of the Douc langur page is also a link. This link brings you back to the zoo collection page.

When using hyperlinks to jump from Web page to Web page, people usually say that they are "going to" those Web pages. In a sense, though, the Web pages are really coming to you as you click on the links and the HTML files are sent to your computer. Nevertheless, it is useful and fun to think of yourself as "visiting" the Web sites you choose.

POINTING AT HYPERLINKS

Most Web pages will have several hyperlinks in them. Occasionally, it may be difficult to tell if a word or picture is a hyperlink. Sometimes you can tell that a picture on a Web page is a hyperlink because it has a special dark border around it. To be sure, you can drag the mouse pointer over the possible hyperlink. If it is a link, the arrow will always change to a pointing finger.

There are Web pages that are made up of almost nothing but hyperlinks. These pages help you find your way around the Web the way an index or table of contents helps you find your way around in a book like this one.

ADDRESSES

How does your Web browser know where to find a file on the Web? Just as a house has an address so people will know how to find it, every file on the Internet has a unique address so that your Web browser will be able to find it. The image on the following page shows the home page for StarChild, a Web site set up by NASA for young astronomers. Below the tool bar is a long

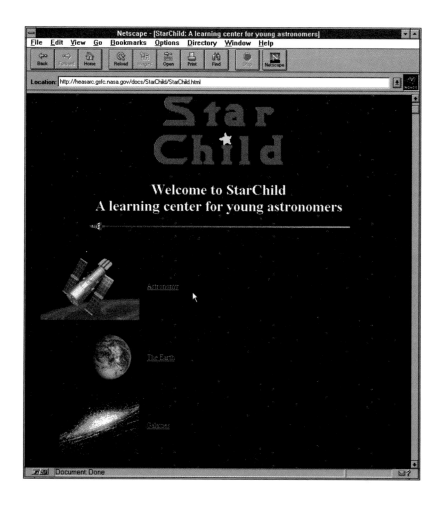

white box labeled "Location" containing the address **http://heasarc.gsfc.nasa.gov/docs/StarChild/StarChild.html**. This is the address, called a *URL* (for Uniform Resource Locator), for the StarChild home page. Each part of the URL gives us information about the file the address points to.

For example, the letters **http** at the beginning of StarChild's URL is an abbreviation for *HyperText Transfer Protocol.* A protocol is a standard method of sending files over the Internet. HyperText Transfer Protocol is the standard method for sending files written in HTML. So the **http** at the beginning of this URL tells the Web browser to expect an HTML file. Other URLs may begin with different protocols. These sites use protocols other than HyperText Transfer Protocol to send files over the Internet. We'll talk more about this later.

The second part of the URL, **heasarc.gsfc.nasa.gov**, is called the *domain name.* This part of the URL tells us several things about the computer that runs the StarChild Web site. For instance, **heasarc.gsfc** is an abbreviation for the High Energy Astrophysics Science Archive Research Center (HEASARC) at the Goddard Space Flight Center (GSFC), which is the division of NASA responsible for the StarChild site. Many other domain names on the World Wide Web begin simply with **www** to indicate that they are Web sites. The next part of the URL, in this case **nasa.gov**, tells us that computer hosting the StarChild Web site is owned by the National Aeronautics and Space Administration (NASA), and that it is a government institution.

Not all domain names end with **gov**. Some end with **com**, which tells us that they are commercial Web sites, probably run by businesses or corporations. Others end with **org**, which tells us that these sites are run by nonprofit organizations, such as charities. The domain names of educational institutions end with **edu**, military sites end with **mil**, and network sites end with **net**. Web sites based in countries other than the United States often have URLs ending in abbreviations that tell us what country they are in. For instance, Web sites in the United Kingdom often have URLs ending with the letters **uk**.

The part of the URL immediately after the domain name, **/docs/StarChild/**, tells NASA's computer where the data file containing the StarChild home page is located on the computer's hard drive.

Everything after the final slash (/) in a URL is the name of the file that contains the information for the home page. Just as the files on your computer's hard disk have names, all of the files on the Web have names. The name of this file is **StarChild.html**. In this case, the file is named after the title of the Web site. The second part of the name, **html**, indicates that the file is written in HyperHext Mark-up Language. This confirms that the file is a Web page.

Not all URLs contain the complete name of the file where the Web page is stored. Some just contain the domain name of the site itself. For instance, the URL for the home page of the *New York Times* Web site (run by the newspaper of the same name) is **http://www.nytimes.com/**. Typing this URL will cause your browser to automatically read a special introductory file stored on the *New York Times* computer.

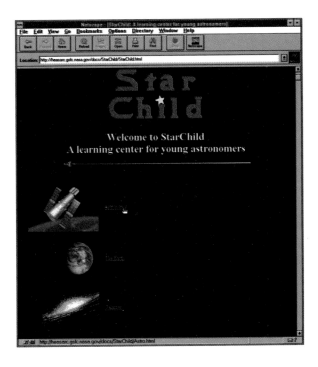

When you point to a hyperlink, the address of the file indicated by the link appears in a status bar at the bottom of the browser window. On the StarChild home page above, notice that the mouse pointer changes into a pointing hand as it is dragged over the <u>Astronomy</u> link. In the status bar at the bottom of the window, you see the address **http://heasarc.gsfc.nasa.gov/docs/StarChild/Astro.html**. This is the address for another page at the StarChild Web site that provides more information about the science of astronomy. Clicking on the link brings us to the astronomy page, shown opposite.

File   Edit   View   Go   Bookmarks   Options   Directory   Window   Help

Back   Forward   Home   Reload   Images   Open   Print   Find   Stop   Netscape

Location: http://heasarc.gsfc.nasa.gov/docs/StarChild/Astro.html

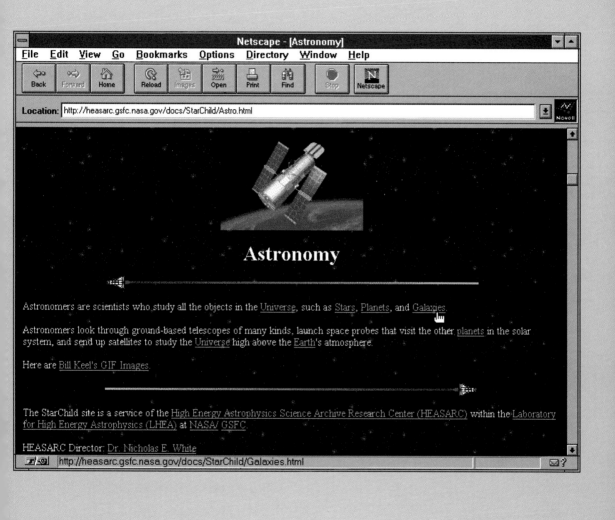

Astronomy

Astronomers are scientists who study all the objects in the Universe, such as Stars, Planets, and Galaxies.

Astronomers look through ground-based telescopes of many kinds, launch space probes that visit the other planets in the solar system, and send up satellites to study the Universe high above the Earth's atmosphere.

Here are Bill Keel's GIF Images.

The StarChild site is a service of the High Energy Astrophysics Science Archive Research Center (HEASARC) within the Laboratory for High Energy Astrophysics (LHEA) at NASA/ GSFC.

HEASARC Director: Dr. Nicholas E. White

http://heasarc.gsfc.nasa.gov/docs/StarChild/Galaxies.html

OTHER PROTOCOLS

One of the reasons why the World Wide Web has become such a popular means of navigating the Internet is that it is very versatile. Web browsers are capable of handling files sent with protocols other than HyperText Transfer Protocol. For example, many sites on the Internet are equipped to send files using a protocol called *ftp*, which stands for *file transfer protocol*. Using your Web browser, you can still download files from these sites. URLs for ftp sites usually look something like this:

ftp://oak.oakland.edu/

Note that the URL begins with the abbreviation **ftp** instead of **http**. This prepares your browser to use the different protocol. The domain name tells us that this is the Oak ftp archive located at Oakland University, which is an educational institution.

Before the World Wide Web became the most popular way to navigate the Internet, many institutions used a system called *gopher*. Gopher, which was developed at the University of Minnesota in 1991, makes it easy to find resources on the Internet by arranging them in a series of *menus*. When you see an entry on a list that looks interesting, you can select it with your mouse, bringing you to a more detailed menu. The menus can also contain files, such as pictures or documents, that you can download with a click of your mouse.

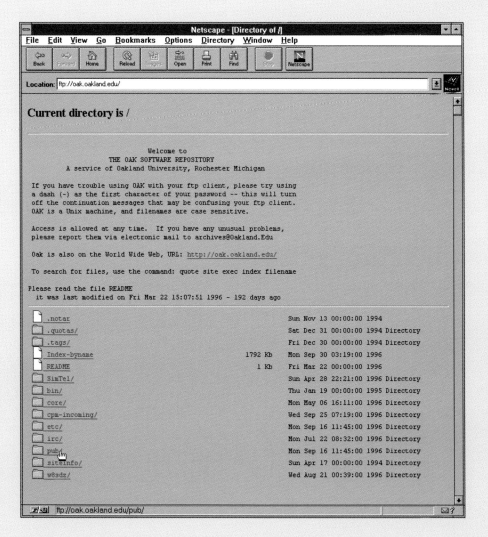

Because Web browsers can understand several protocols, they can connect to ftp archives such as this one at Oakland University.

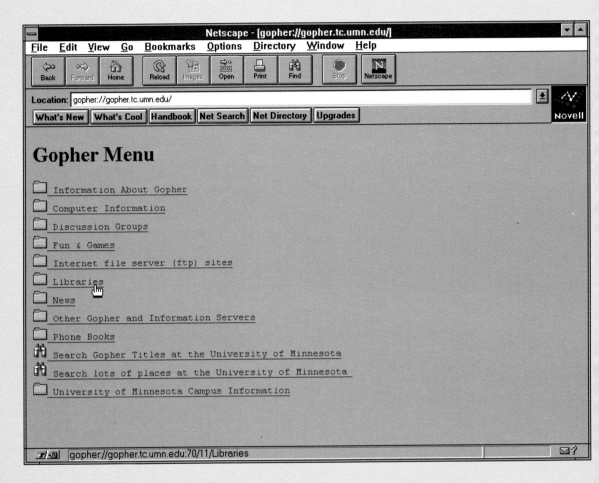

Web browsers can also connect to gopher sites, such as this one at the University of Minnesota.

Many institutions that have not yet created Web sites maintain gopher sites, and you can visit them with your Web browser. Gopher URLs look like this:

gopher://gopher.tc.umn.edu/

The word **gopher** at the beginning of the URL tells the browser to expect to connect to a gopher site. The rest tells us that this is an educational site located at the University of Minnesota (UMN).

USING URLS

Most of the time, you'll find your way around on the Web by clicking on hyperlinks. Any hyperlink that points to a Web page automatically tells the Web browser the address of that Web page. Following links, however, is not the only way to navigate around the Web. It is also possible to jump to a particular site by entering the URL directly. You can tell your Web browser to take you to a specific URL by pulling down the "File" menu at the top of the screen and selecting an option with a name like "Open Location…" Or you can type the URL in the long box below the Web browser's toolbar and then press the Return (or Enter) key. In both cases, the Web browser will then take you to the page on the Web that has that URL. When entering URLs, pay close attention to symbols and capital and lowercase letters; URLs must be entered exactly as they appear.

So, suppose you've run your Web browser and you want to go to the Web site run by LucasArts Entertainment, a company that publishes many computer games. You just choose "Open Location..." (or something similar) and a little window, called a *dialog box,* will appear on your screen. Type **http://www.lucasarts.com/menu.html** in the dialog box and press the Return (or Enter) key. Presto! You'll be transported to the LucasArts Entertainment Web site, where you can read all about their games.

BOOKMARKS

Typing URLs can get pretty boring, so most Web browsers allow you to keep lists of your favorite URLs. Once you've stored a URL in this list, all you have to do to get to that site again is open up a menu and click on its name. In Netscape Navigator, this list of favorite URLs is called Bookmarks, and you can find it in the "Bookmarks" menu.

BACK AND FORTH

If you go to a Web page and then decide that you'd rather be back at the page you were on before, don't panic. Near the upper left-hand corner of your Web browser's screen you'll probably see a couple of arrows, one pointing right and one pointing left. Just click on the arrow pointing to the left and you'll be automatically returned to the last page you were on. In fact, you can keep clicking on this arrow until you're all the way back at the first page that you visited.

If you accidentally go too far and want to go back to the page you just returned from, click on the arrow pointing to the right to go in the opposite direction.

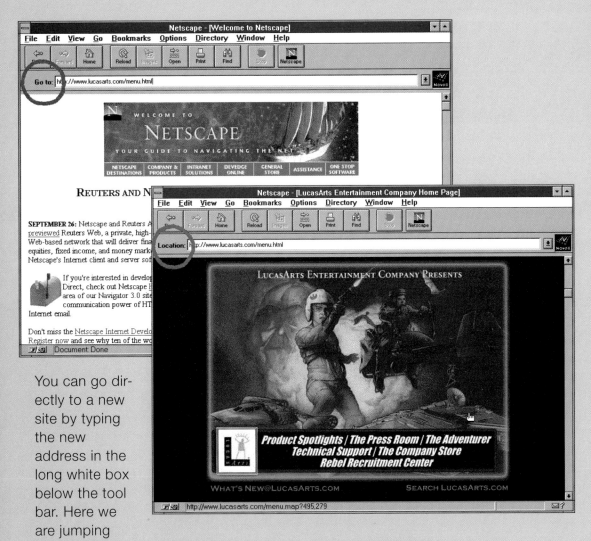

You can go directly to a new site by typing the new address in the long white box below the tool bar. Here we are jumping from the Netscape Web site to the LucasArts Entertainment Web site by typing the LucasArts address in the box. Notice that as you type the address, the label beside the box changes from "Location" to "Go to." Once the new page has been retrieved, the label switches back to "Location."

IS IT BROKEN?

Web browsers can be slow. Sometimes it can seem to take forever to go from one Web page to another. You might be tempted to wonder if your browser is broken. If so, look in the upper right-hand corner of the browser's screen. You'll see a small box with an animated picture in it. This picture may show a spinning globe or falling meteorites—or just about anything else. If this picture is moving, then your browser is still working.

Occasionally your browser won't be able to reach the Web page you just told it to go to. Perhaps the computer that contains the file for that page is having a problem or the URL you typed for the page is incorrect. Sometimes the page simply isn't there anymore. When this happens, the browser will eventually quit trying to go to the page and will display an error message telling you what went wrong.

This can take a long time, though. If you get bored waiting, there should be a button on your browser's toolbar that tells it to stop trying. This button may look like a little stop sign or just a red circle. Click on it and your browser will give up its search for the next page and let you do something else instead.

OH, THE PLACES YOU'LL GO!

Now that you've learned how to get on the Web and how to move around once you're on it, where should you go? The answer is— just about any place you want to go! In the next chapter, we'll look at how to find interesting places on the Web.

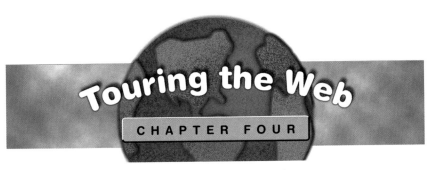

Touring the Web

CHAPTER FOUR

Okay, you've just run your Web browser. It's waiting for you to tell it where to go. What Web site should you visit first?

That's up to you, of course. You may be in the mood to read about the latest movies and TV shows, download a demo of the cool new computer game you just heard about, or maybe just look at interesting pictures. If you know about a Web site that features some of these things, type in the URL and go there.

Of course, you may not know the URL of any place like that. So what do you do then?

You may want to check out a *Web index.*

WEB INDEXES

Web indexes are Web sites that are made up mostly of hyperlinks to other Web sites. A good Web index can help you find your way around on the Web, even if you don't know exactly where you're going.

One of the best Web indexes is called Yahoo. You can reach Yahoo by typing the URL **http://www.yahoo.com/** on your Web browser. When you get there, you'll see a screen that lists a lot of different subjects, such as entertainment and

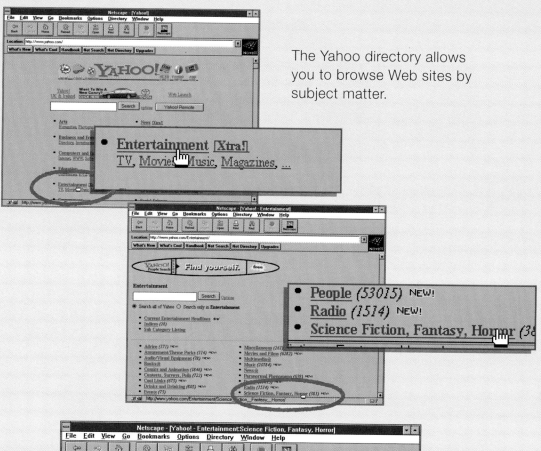

The Yahoo directory allows you to browse Web sites by subject matter.

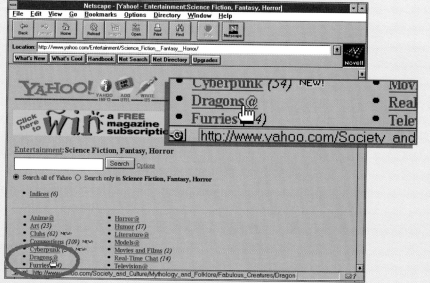

computers. When you click on one of these subjects, you'll go to another index page.

For instance, if you click on the <u>Entertainment</u> link, you get an index of entertainment-related topics. Now suppose you click on the link <u>Science Fiction, Fantasy, Horror</u>. This takes you to still another list. This list is actually two different lists—one of additional subtopics, such as <u>Dragons</u>, and one of the names of actual Web sites. Click on the name of one of the Web sites and you'll go to that site. Click on a subtopic and you'll go to yet another list of topics and sites.

The index at Yahoo is huge and contains links to thousands of Web sites listed under hundreds of different topics.

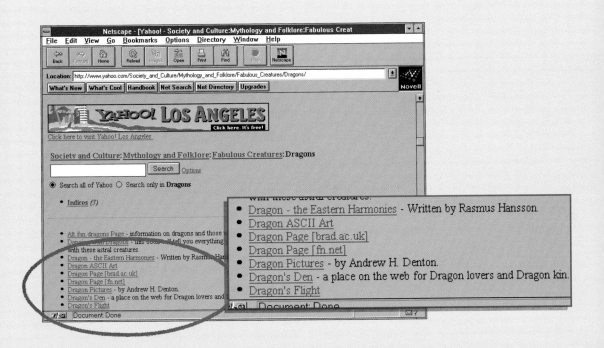

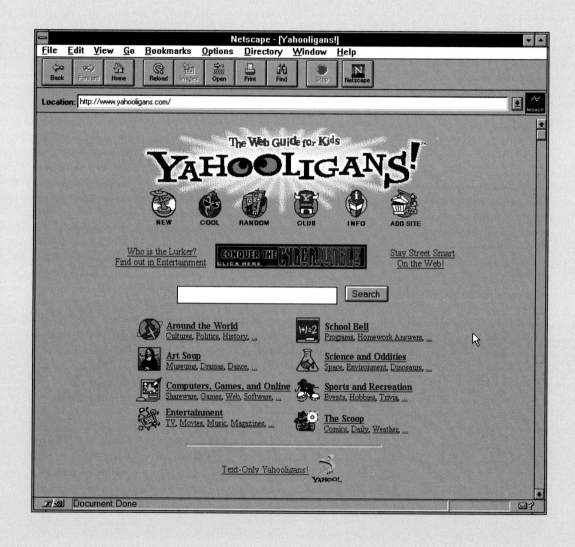

It shouldn't be hard to find what you're looking for at Yahoo. And if Yahoo doesn't have what you want, keep your eyes open for other indexes as you explore the Web. You'll probably discover quite a few, many of them with lists of sites on specific topics. In fact, Yahoo will even give you the names of other Web indexes.

Yahoo also maintains a Web index especially for kids. It is called Yahooligans and can be reached at **http://www.yahooligans.com/**. Yahooligans works exactly like the main Yahoo index, but it contains only sites of interest to kids.

SEARCH ENGINES

Another way to find what you're looking for on the Web is to use computer programs on the Web called *search engines*. Many search engines will search the entire Web for you to find sites containing certain words. For instance, if you want to find a site that contains the words "sports scores," you would type those words into the search engine and tell it to look for them. (Some search engines will require that you put quotes around the words to show that they go together. Others may require that you put the word "and" between the two words so it knows you're looking for a site that contains both words instead of just either one of them. Check the search engine's instructions to find out for sure.)

The search engine will then give you a list of hyperlinks to all or some of the sites containing the words you're looking for. You can then click on those links to go to the sites.

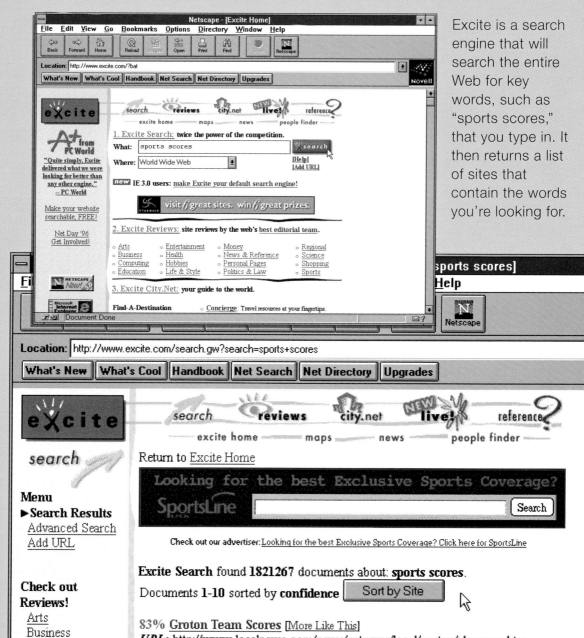

Excite is a search engine that will search the entire Web for key words, such as "sports scores," that you type in. It then returns a list of sites that contain the words you're looking for.

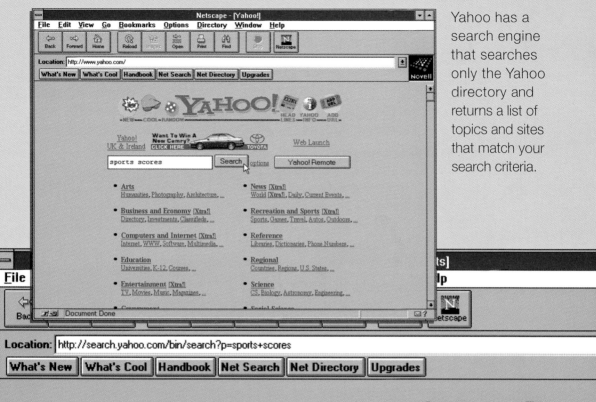

Yahoo has a search engine that searches only the Yahoo directory and returns a list of topics and sites that match your search criteria.

Location: http://search.yahoo.com/bin/search?p=sports+scores

What's New | **What's Cool** | **Handbook** | **Net Search** | **Net Directory** | **Upgrades**

My Yahoo! - Net Events - Stock Quotes - Yahoo! SF Bay - Weekly Picks

PCWEEK — **Hear the latest computing news!** ZDNet

Found 292 matches containing **sports scores**. Displaying matches 1-20.

Yahoo Categories - **Yahoo Sites** - AltaVista Web Pages

Yahoo Categories

Recreation:**Sports**:Baseball:Major League Baseball (MLB):**Scores**

Yahoo Sites

Other search engines are dedicated to individual Web sites and will direct you to specific pages within a site that contain words you've searched for. Yahoo, for example, features a search engine that will search the Yahoo index and give you a list of hyperlinks that match the words you've searched for. To find sites that are not included in the Yahoo index, Yahoo lists some popular search engines that will search the rest of the Web.

Here's a list of some of the most popular Web-wide search engines:

WebCrawler	http://www.webcrawler.com/
Alta Vista	http://www.altavista.com/
Lycos	http://www.lycos.com/
Infoseek	http://www.infoseek.com/
Excite	http://www.excite.com/

Many of these search engines have their own Web indexes attached. Although you can get to each of these engines by using its URL, you'll also find links to these search engines at many other sites.

Finally, if you keep your eyes open, you can learn URLs from places other than the Web—and not just in this book! Newspaper and magazine articles often mention the URLs for interesting Web sites—so do TV ads and shows. Keep a list of the URLs you read, see, and hear about, and pretty soon you'll have a Web index of your own!

Still not sure where you want to go on the Web? In the next chapter, we'll look at some interesting sites to help you get started.

Sites on the Web

Where should you go on the Web? That depends on why you're there in the first place. Maybe you're looking for help with your homework. You can use Web sites to do research for schoolwork the same way you use books at the library. Having the Web on your computer is like having access to the biggest library on earth!

MUSEUMS

A good place to start getting information is a museum, and there are a lot of museums on the Web. If you think a museum is a dry and uninteresting place, you'll be pleasantly surprised with Web museums. They're jam-packed with information about things you'll find both fascinating and useful, from dinosaurs and space travel to rock music and comic strips. And you just might learn some cool things about history, geography, and science along the way!

One of the most important museums on earth is the Smithsonian Institution, which is actually an assortment of many different museums. In the real world, you have to go to Washington, D.C., to find the Smithsonian, but you'll find its home page at **http://www.si.edu/**. Click on a few of the

The Smithsonian
Institution Web
site provides a
map of the Mall in
Washington, D.C.

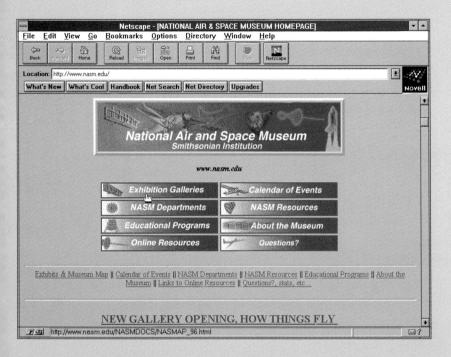

Clicking on any of the individual museums on the Smithsonian map takes you to their home pages, such as these for the National Air and Space Museum and the National Museum of Natural History.

hypertext buttons on this page and you'll be off to any of eighteen different Smithsonian museums.

Are you interested in airplanes and rockets? Then head straight for the National Air and Space Museum—on the Web, that is. You can reach it through the Smithsonian home page or directly at **http://www.nasm.edu/**. Maybe you'll see an exhibition on Rocketry and Space Flight or on World War II Aviation.

For something a little more down to earth, hop over to the National Museum of American History at **http://www. si.edu/organiza/museums/nmah/homepage/nmah.htm**. At this site, you can see the flag that flew over Fort McHenry the night the Star Spangled Banner was written, as well as an exhibit of historic computers.

Another great Smithsonian museum is the National Museum of Natural History at **http://nmnhwww.si.edu/nmnhweb.html**, where you'll encounter whales, cave people, dinosaurs, and gemstones.

There are plenty of other museums on the Web. Any good Web index or search engine will tell you where they are.

ART GALLERIES

Do you want to see some of the greatest art ever created? Go straight to the greatest art gallery in the world, the Louvre in Paris. The official Louvre Web site is located at **http://mistral.culture.fr/louvre/louvrea.htm**. Here you can see, among others, one of the most famous paintings of all time: the Mona Lisa by Leonardo DaVinci.

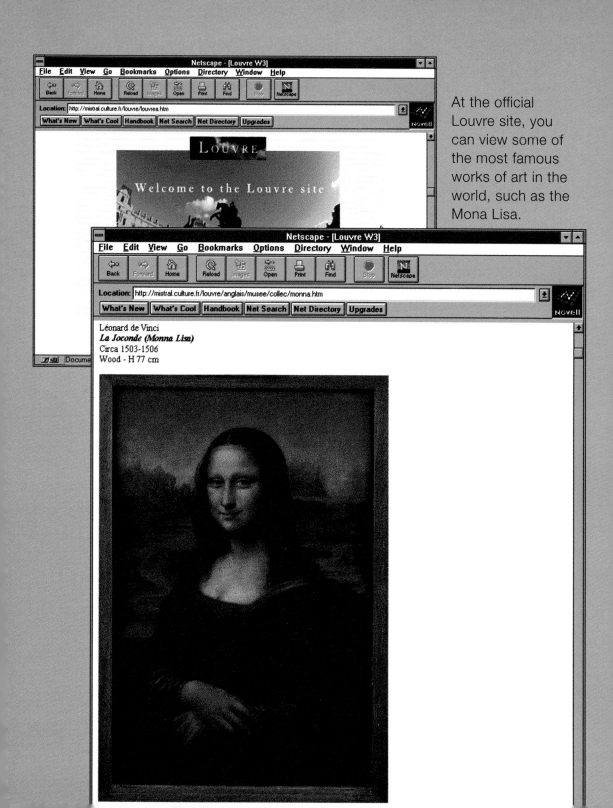

At the official Louvre site, you can view some of the most famous works of art in the world, such as the Mona Lisa.

Léonard de Vinci
La Joconde (Monna Lisa)
Circa 1503-1506
Wood - H 77 cm

The White House Web site

One thing to notice about art museums on the Web, as well as about a lot of other sites that contain pictures, is that they use a lot of *thumbnails*. A thumbnail is a tiny version of a picture that, when clicked on with your mouse pointer, becomes a larger picture. If the Mona Lisa seems awfully small, click on her to get a better look. (Don't do this at a *real* art gallery, of course.)

GOVERNMENT SITES

The U.S. government, and most local governments, have put up Web sites of their own. If you want to go right to the top, take a private tour of the White House and surrounding parts of Washington, D.C., at **http://www.whitehouse.gov/**. Whether you have a homework assignment about the Executive Branch of the government or are just curious about the house where the President of the United States lives, this is the Web site to visit. There are copies of important documents and speeches, pictures of the First Family, and even a history of the U.S. Presidency.

The U.S. Senate also has a site, at **http://www.senate.gov/**. Here you can learn who your elected representatives are, what laws they've passed, and take a trip around the U.S. Capitol building. The House of Representatives has a similar site at—you guessed it—**http://www.house.gov/**.

All three of these sites—the White House, the Senate, and the House of Representatives—let you leave comments for your elected representatives so you can tell them how you think they're doing. If you have an opinion, don't hesitate to let them know about it, but try to be polite.

COMMERCIAL SITES

The truth is that most of the bigger Web sites are commercial sites—that is, they were put up by somebody who is usually trying to sell you something. There's nothing wrong with that, of course. But when you visit a site that has a URL ending in **com**, you should remember that it's essentially an advertisement, much like the ones you see on TV. When they tell you that their product is the greatest in the world, chances are you'll find another site somewhere telling you that some other product is even better.

A lot of time and money goes into putting up a commercial Web site, so they can be a lot of fun. They usually have attractive artwork, cleverly written text, and interesting gimmicks—like games and music you can play online. (You may need special programs that work with your Web browser to play the games and music, but these programs can usually be downloaded right off the Web.)

Name a famous company and chances are that it has a site on the Web. For instance, there are software publishers, movie studios, television networks, automobile manufacturers, electronics companies (and lots of them!), airlines, shoe companies, and soda bottlers.

It's easy to find most commercial sites because they almost always have **www** at the beginning of their URL, **com** at the end, and the name of the company in the middle.

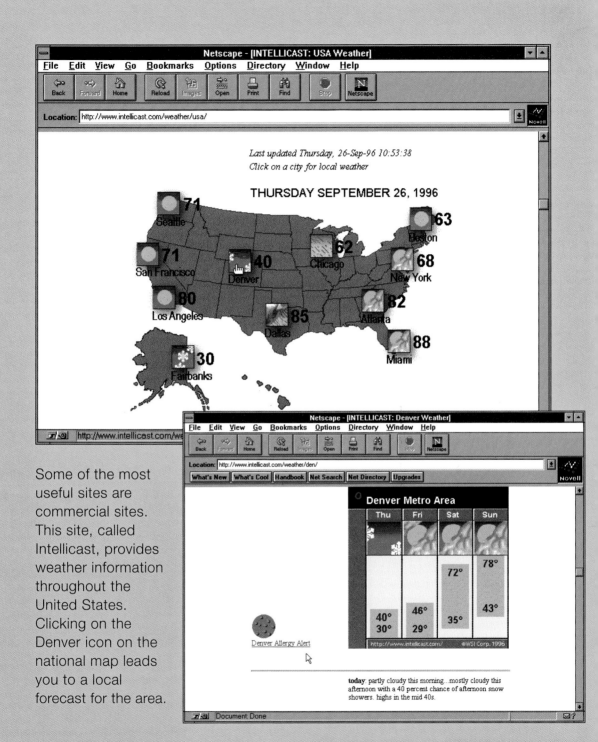

Some of the most useful sites are commercial sites. This site, called Intellicast, provides weather information throughout the United States. Clicking on the Denver icon on the national map leads you to a local forecast for the area.

Are you interested in reading about software from the Microsoft Corporation? Then go to **http://www.microsoft.com/**. Enjoy Disney movies? You'll find out more about them at **http://www.disney.com/**. Crave the taste of Coca-Cola? Then visit **http://www.cocacola.com/**.

Of course, big corporations want to be absolutely sure you know the names of their Web sites. So look at the bottom of almost any ad these days in the newspaper (and sometimes on television) and you'll see the URL of the Web site devoted to that sponsor. And if you *still* can't find the company you're looking for, don't forget Web indexes and search engines.

YOUR FAVORITE SHOWS AND STARS

Do you have a favorite performer—a singer or a popular actress, perhaps—and want to know more about him or her than you can learn at a commercial site? Chances are there's a Web page devoted to this person, maybe several. Unfortunately, you usually can't guess the names of these Web sites the way you can with commercial sites. Most pages devoted to performers are created for fun by fans much like yourself.

So how do you find these pages? Just the way you'd expect: through Web indexes and search engines.

Same goes for TV shows. Many popular shows have several pages devoted to them. Look up "Star Trek" using a search engine and you'll find lots of pages. Check them out and learn the difference between a Borg and a Ferengi.

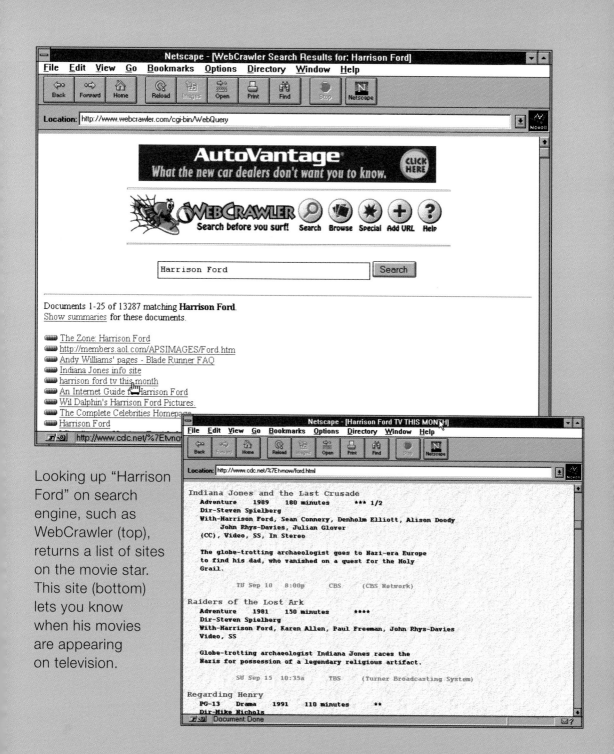

Looking up "Harrison Ford" on search engine, such as WebCrawler (top), returns a list of sites on the movie star. This site (bottom) lets you know when his movies are appearing on television.

IT'S A BIG, BIG WEB!

There are several types of Web pages we haven't even had time to discuss here—and literally millions of pages we haven't named. But that really doesn't matter. The Web is about exploration. It's about finding things on your own. One of the coolest things about the Web is that you can start out looking for one thing and discover a dozen other things you didn't even know you were interested in.

The list in this chapter should be enough to get you started, but now you're on your own. Have fun! You've got a big journey ahead of you!

Author's Note

The Web is pretty new. It's only been around for a few years and it's still changing quickly. So some of the sites mentioned in this book might have moved by the time you read this. Although the author of this book has tried to choose only sites that will probably stay in the same places for a very long time, some of the URLs given on previous pages may not work.

If this happens, don't give up! If you've been reading carefully, you'll know exactly what to do. Here's a hint: it has something to do with Web indexes and search engines.

Web browsers are changing too. New versions of both Netscape Navigator and Microsoft Internet Explorer come out every few months, and other Web browsers appear all the time. But chances are the one you have will work pretty much like the ones described in this book.

Glossary

account – a contract with an Internet service provider that allows you to connect to the Internet through their computers.

data files – the form in which information, including computer programs, is stored on your computer's disk drive(s).

dialog box – a little window that appears on your computer screen to tell you something important or request that you enter information.

domain name – the part of a URL that tells your Web browser about the computer that stores the Web files.

download – to transfer programs and other special files from the Internet to your computer's hard drive or to a diskette.

files – see data files

file transfer protocol (ftp) – the standard protocol for downloading files from special ftp sites on the Internet.

gopher – a part of the Internet where files and other resources are arranged according to a system of menus.

graphical Web browser – a Web browser that allows pictures to be displayed in a Web page. Most Web browsers are graphical browsers.

hard drive – a permanent, magnetic disk inside your computer that stores computer programs and other types of information so that you can access them easily.

home page – the introductory page of a Web site or a page that your browser automatically loads when you first log on to the Web.

HTML – short for HyperText Markup Language, this is the form in which most files on the World Wide Web are written.

hyperlink – a word or image representing a connection between one part of the World Wide Web and another part.

HyperText Transfer Protocol (HTTP) – the standard method for sending HTML files over the Internet.

Internet – a group of computers around the world that are connected together in such a way that each can send messages to the others.

Internet service provider – a company that provides Internet service to individuals, businesses, and institutions.

menu – a list of options on a computer that can be selected by clicking the mouse or pressing the Enter key.

modem – a device that connects your computer to a telephone line so that it can communicate with computers in other locations.

search engines – computer programs on the Web that allow you to search for pages containing words that you specify.

servers – computers, permanently connected to the Internet, that provide services to other computers.

text file – a type of computer file that contains words, numbers, and symbols.

thumbnail – a tiny picture on a Web page that, when clicked on, is replaced by a larger version of the same picture.

URL – short for Uniform Resource Locator, this is the "address" of a Web page and is how your computer finds a page on the Web.

Web browser – a program that reads files written in HTML and displays them on your computer screen with formatted text and pictures.

Web index – a site on the Web that consists mostly of hyperlinks to other sites.

Web page – an HTML file when it's viewed using a Web browser.

Web site – a collection of Web pages stored on an Internet computer where they can be read by your Web browser.

World Wide Web – a large collection of files on the Internet that are connected by hyperlinks. The information can be accessed using a computer and a Web browser.

Index

About the Author

Noted science writer Christopher Lampton has written more than seventy-five books on subjects such as astronomy, computers, genetic engineering, meteorology, and the environment. He is the author of the best-selling *Flights of Fantasy*, about advanced computer game programming. In addition to his nonfiction, he has written several science fiction novels, as well as adventure novels for young adults. Mr. Lampton holds a degree in broadcast communications, and he makes his home in Gaithersburg, Maryland.